The
SPUR BOOK
of
DINGHY CRUISING

The
SPUR BOOK
of
DINGHY CRUISING

by
Margaret Dye

With Illustrations by
Terry Brown

SPURBOOKS LIMITED

Published 1977 by
SPURBOOKS LTD.
6 Parade Court
Bourne End
Bucks

ISBN 0 904978 68 0

Printed by Maund & Irvine, Ltd., Tring, Herts.

CONTENTS

INTRODUCTION

ABOUT THIS SERIES

Venture Guides are written to provide outdoor people of all persuasions, sailors, climbers, campers, snorkellers, backpackers, with a range of information on basic skills, and additional techniques and pastimes. They cover such skills as Map Reading, Camping, First Aid, Weather Lore, and Survival techniques. Other titles cover Sailing, Back Packing, Rock Climbing, Hill-trekking, and now, the subject of this book, Dinghy Cruising.

ABOUT THIS BOOK

It has been said, with truth, that to learn how to get the best from your boat you must race it as well as cruise it, so that there exists a vast and growing library on all aspects of dinghy racing, while books on keel-boat cruising flow onto the market in a steady flood.

Less attention has been given to the popular and growing pastime of dinghy cruising, but this too has its devotees, and of them, no couple is better known than Frank Dye and his wife Margaret, who together have notched up some notable cruises in their 16' Wayfarer *'Wanderer'*.

Margaret Dye is also Cruising Secretary of the Wayfarer Association, and in this book she records her advice for those people who want to start cruising in dinghies. (Please study Terry Brown's drawings as they contain lots of information as well.)

Many people enjoy the challenge of racing dinghies, but others find little satisfaction in racing around buoys, finding perhaps, enough stress in the pressures of everyday life. For such people, cruising is a complete relaxation, and small boat cruising provides the opportunity to learn and practise a wide range of sailing and other outdoor skills, as well as getting bags of fresh air and driven spray!

Chapter 1

HOW TO START

You need a well-found dinghy! Many dinghies can race, day cruise, or potter about to their owner's complete content, but if the original aim when purchasing a dinghy is to cruise in it, then the prospective purchaser needs to have certain features in mind when looking for a suitable boat.

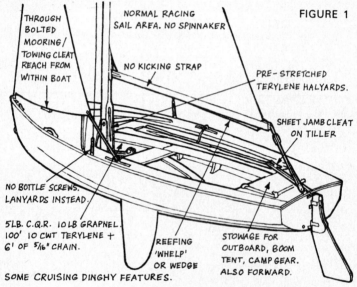

FIGURE 1

THROUGH BOLTED MOORING/TOWING CLEAT REACH FROM WITHIN BOAT

NORMAL RACING SAIL AREA. NO SPINNAKER

NO KICKING STRAP

PRE-STRETCHED TERYLENE HALYARDS.

SHEET JAMB CLEAT ON TILLER

NO BOTTLE SCREWS. LANYARDS INSTEAD.

5LB. C.Q.R. 10LB GRAPNEL. 100' 10 CWT TERYLENE + 6' OF 5/16" CHAIN.

REEFING 'WHELP' OR WEDGE

STOWAGE FOR OUTBOARD, BOOM TENT, CAMP GEAR. ALSO FORWARD.

SOME CRUISING DINGHY FEATURES.

WHY A DINGHY?

Many people think that the right boat for cruising has to be a cabined keel-boat. This is not necessarily the case, and they have in mind a different type of cruising. Dinghy cruising may not be better than keel-boat cruising, but it is different, and has enjoyments and challenges peculiar to itself, and one great advantage—mobility.

Towed on a trailer, you can take your dinghy to a different cruising ground every weekend. You can explore shallow creeks, lakes and winding rivers. You can camp and cook in the fresh air, and pit yourself, in an open boat, against the elements. Moreover, as my husband, Frank, has demonstrated, dinghies, well-found and competently crewed, can sail almost anywhere, and dinghy cruising is fun.

PHYSICAL SKILLS AND MENTAL APPROACH

Physically, there are few limitations, and provided you are prepared to experiment, be cautious and adaptable, and willing to gain experience *slowly,* you will soon develop those additional skills that enable people to cover distances in small boats. Remember that ten miles in a dinghy can be as big an adventure as a hundred miles in a large yacht. You will need to know, or learn about quite a number of outdoor skills, some of which may not, at first sight, seem relevant to the sea.

The dinghy-cruising sailor needs, apart from a good grasp of dayboat handling, a good knowledge of navigation, cookery, camping, weather lore, first aid, and natural history. I shall cover, or touch upon most of these activities in this book. The more you can learn about all of them, the better off you will be. The scope for learning new skills is enormous, as are the opportunities for making friends in the out-of-the-way places you can get to in a small boat. You will find all these activities enjoyable.

CHOICE OF CRAFT

High performance dinghies are not ideal for cruising. They are generally too 'tender', lack stowage room and, while ideal for their racing role, are too refined to be easily adapted for cruising.

When looking for a cruising dinghy, look for the following points:—

1. L.O.A. between 14-18 feet. Anything smaller is too small, anything larger is hard to beach and trail.

2. Ample beam, to give stability, and of double chine construction—which I prefer, as I consider it to be very stable.

3. Centre board, rather than dagger-board.

4. Ample freeboard: This keeps the boat dry in a rough sea.

5. Flat floorboards: This keeps small items from getting wet or lost in the bilge, and you can sleep on them, above the bilgewater.

6. Good fore and side-decks, for sitting on and working from.

7. Ample stowage, fore, aft, and in the cockpit.

8. Good buoyancy characteristics.

9. Proved, sound construction, able to resist bad weather and rough handling on the beach.
10. Not too heavy.

I could go on and on, listing more points or simply recommending my own preferences, the *Wayfarer,* or *Gull* dinghies, or the *Drascombe* range, but let's look at a few of these points in more detail.

WOOD OR G.R.P.

Wood is easier to adapt than G.R.P., but needs more maintenance. Screwing and gluing of shelving and lockers is easier with a wooden boat, and the wooden hull stands up better to regular beaching. G.R.P. scratches easily on shingle, the gel-coat can be damaged, and G.R.P. craft are more difficult to fit out. A wooden boat has natural buoyancy, and a high asthetic value. Our original wooden *Wayfarer* has just been replaced by an identical boat, so you can understand that I would always recommend wood, but many people cruise happily in G.R.P. craft, which give more sailing for less maintenance.

HULL

Sea-worthiness and stability depend on no small measure to the hull construction. Flat-bottomed beamy boats should attract the cruising helmsman's eye, rather than a narrow, sleek, racing hull. Clinker construction takes beaching well, but clinker boats are heavy to handle ashore. Carvel-built boats also tend to be heavy for their size, and often leak as they age. Double-chine hulls, like the *Wayfarer,* are sea-worthy and have good on-shore handling characteristics, and are my recommendation. A foredeck is a good hull feature, as it gives stowage space and provides a working area. Side decks make sitting out more comfortable.

RIG

I think the Bermuda rig gives the best all-round cruising performance, and they are especially good to windward. Lug and gaff rigs are also popular with cruising folk, and are certainly good downwind, although less effective on other points of sailing.

The cruising helm needs an easy, well-balanced rig. He needs the ability to reef easily, by either roller reefing, jiffy reefing, or reefing points on the sail. Again the Bermuda rig scores well here.

Some of my cruising friends maintain that a lower rig, like gaff or gunter is better for cruising for the mast and spars being shorter, can be lashed in the boat while trailing, the boat is more stable at anchor and the mast is simple to step.

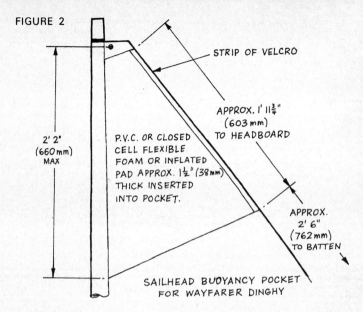

FIGURE 2

STRIP OF VELCRO

APPROX. 1' 11¾"
(603 mm)
TO HEADBOARD

2' 2"
(660mm)
MAX

P.V.C. OR CLOSED
CELL FLEXIBLE
FOAM OR INFLATED
PAD APPROX. 1½" (38mm)
THICK INSERTED
INTO POCKET.

APPROX.
2' 6"
(762 mm)
TO BATTEN

SAILHEAD BUOYANCY POCKET
FOR WAYFARER DINGHY

STABILITY

It is extremely important that a cruising dinghy is as stable as possible. A capsize in a tidal estuary or on the open sea can be a real problem. Stability largely depends on proper seamanship, prompt and adequate reefing, good stowage, correct helm work etc. However, a beamy boat is less likely to capsize than a light one. A short mast is more stable, especially at anchor.

The risk of a fully inverted capsize can be reduced by putting buoyancy at the mast top. Wooden masts are inherently buoyant, but I know people who put a fender on the top of their metal mast to prevent it from going right under, which is a good idea. Adding ballast in the shape of crew or stores, also increases stability.

RAISING AND LOWERING THE MAST UNDER WAY

Cruising inland, you need to raise and lower the mast to get under bridges and power wires. The forestay and shrouds can have rope extensions, and the mast can be dropped back in a tabernacle, 'all standing'. Remember to release the jib-hanks though, or one will be sure to tear the jib. Lower the mast, away from any power lines crossing the river, or you may disappear in a brilliant electrical flash!

11

Bottle-screws for tensioning the shrouds are fine for racing, but for cruising they can and should be replaced with less expensive, more serviceable and very handy lengths of pre-stretched terylene lanyards. Many dinghy sailors cruising on inshore waters prefer gaff or gunter rigs because the mast is easier to lower—and usually lower anyway.

KICKING STRAP
In spite of its designed advantages, a kicking strap is often a practical disadvantage on a cruising dinghy. On long tacks there is less need for one, so it is best to just carry it in the stores, fitting it when needed, which is usually on the downwind passages. You should also know how to roll the sail-bag, into the reefed mainsail, to serve as a kicking strap, in heavier weather.

SHEET-HORSE
A centre main-sheet takes over some of the work of the kicking strap, but clutters up the boat if you have to move about much. Generally, if the crew is only two people, a centre main-sheet is more convenient, and leaves more space for gear in the aft of the cockpit. The *Wayfarer* has the sheet-horse on the transom though, and that works out fine as well. It's not a major point.

JAMMING CLEATS
On passage, jamming cleats for main and genoa, take a lot of the strain, but they must be well positioned, and release at a flick. A stuck cleat in a loaded dinghy can be risky.

GOOSENECK AND BOOM FITTINGS
These need constant attention since the usual pottering and light racing fittings are not robust enough for cruising. Fit heavy-duty fittings and carry spares as well.

SAILS
Main, genoa and working jib gives you an adequate rig. You must be able to do simple repairs to the sails if need be, and carry sail repair equipment.

This is the basic boat without extras. You will need quite a lot of other gear and equipment, but before we go on to that, let's look at the personal qualities, the skills needed, and the training available.

Chapter 2

KNOWLEDGE, TRAINING, EXPERIENCE

You will need all three at some time, but probably not to begin with. However, it would be a very foolish sailor who just puts his sleeping bag into the dinghy and sails out of the harbour.

KNOWLEDGE

What do you need to know? Remember that when you go dinghy cruising, you will be sailing on your own, not in a club race, or busy harbour, where friends and rescue-craft are close to hand. You have to look after yourself, and you do need some experience.

Have you:
1. Racing and/or day-sailing experience, so that you can handle your craft competently, including rowing and engine work?
2. Camping skills; can you sleep and cook, out of doors?
3. The ability to read a chart, understand tides and buoyage; can you plot a course?
4. A knowledge of weather lore?
5. The ability to carry out simple repairs to hull, sails and equipment?
6. A knowledge of First Aid?

If you have all this knowledge, much of which is incidentally contained in other books published in this series, then you have a very good basis for your cruising ventures. If not, you must cruise with an experienced sailor, at least to start with.

R.Y.A. COURSES

All R.Y.A. courses, especially those held at the National Sailing Centre at Cowes, are well worth attending. The grounding they give in all aspects of sailing is quite excellent.

Evening classes in seamanship and navigation are also worth attending. Going to a R.Y.A. recognised sailing school to improve one's practical sailing ability, and going to evening classes to improve your theoretical knowledge will back up the time spent with one's boat.

CRUISING IN COMPANY

Rallies organized by the various class associations and the Dinghy Cruising Association are promoted to help the inexperienced cruising family and provide the opportunity to link with sailors who are more experienced. Their help and advice will be useful and will really stick in your mind.

Dinghy Cruising Association, 7 Rogerson Close, Cowes, Isle of Wight, Hants.

Wayfarer Association, M. Dye, 72 Brown Street, Macclesfield, Cheshire SK11 6RY.

Write to the Cruising Secretary of your class association for details.

If you are 'unclubbable' then I think that before you start cruising, especially offshore, you should have the following experience:—

1. A season's crewing and/or helming in sheltered waters, preferably in your own dinghy.

2. A week's course, preferably in day-boat handling at a R.Y.A. approved school.

3. Some cruising experience, perhaps as a crew member on a cabin yacht or keel boat.

4. Extensive reading, study or instruction in navigation, buoyage, safety.

5. Camping and cooking skills—and last, but not least:—

6. The boat must be equipped against all conceivable hazards.

CREWING

One excellent way of gaining experience is to crew for somebody else.

To benefit from this, have an enjoyable time, (and be asked again), I offer you the following advice:—

1. There can be only one skipper on board. Don't argue with him.

2. Do *more* than 50% of the work.

3. Anticipate the needs of the skipper i.e., in getting anchor or fenders ready, or by offering to brew-up or make a sandwich.

4. When you are sailing *his* boat, do it as well and as gently as possible. Be sure you know how to get him back if he falls overboard.

5. Keep your sense of humour.

When on your own, *never* do more than you feel you are capable of doing. Start with day cruising, then try an overnight stop, building up gradually to longer trips and voyages.

There is a lot to learn about small boat cruising, and experience is the best, indeed the only way of learning all the hundred and one tips and wrinkles that you need to know at times. However, we can make a start. But first where shall we go?

Chapter 3

WHERE TO CRUISE

The great advantage the dinghy sailor has over the cabin-yachtsman is MOBILITY. You can cruise virtually anywhere, and drive to the launch site, with the dinghy on the trailer. No long passages to the chosen area for us!

Only native caution and commonsense need inhibit you. You can sail everywhere, but you shouldn't sail anywhere if it isn't safe to do so.

LAUNCHING SITES

The first problem, having trailed the dinghy to the chosen area, is to get it in the water. You can identify likely launching sites off the O.S. map. O.S. maps are, incidentally, invaluable to the dinghy cruising sailor. It is usually possible to get afloat from any beach, hard or harbour. The real problem is access to them, getting permission to launch, and finding somewhere secure to leave car and trailer in your absence. There is a paperback called *'Getting Afloat'* published annually by Link House, which lists over 1500 launching sites all over the U.K. and you should buy a copy at once.

SAILING AREAS

Few places in England are more than a hundred miles from the coast, and motorways greatly assist a speedy journey to the sea. Lakes and non-tidal stretches of rivers allow easy access to the land. If the camp sites are too noisy, it is a simple matter to push off, and anchor offshore. (The mosquitos are less difficult there too!) The Norfolk Broads, Lake District, many Scottish Lochs, the Upper Thames and the Fenland rivers provide much to explore. Estuaries, harbours and tidal rivers mean that sea-worthy dinghies have a new dimension to add to their travelling. The lower Thames, the Solent, the Fal, Plymouth, Conway, the Menai Straits, the Humber, the Dart, the Severn, the Dee, the Clyde, and the Firth of Forth, and all the tidal rivers in Suffolk and Essex—not to mention abroad—mean that, in a lifetime, there will always be a new tide to sail on.

COASTAL SAILING

Coastal sailing often involves the hard decision of knowing when *not* to go! A Force-4 wind on an inland lake is a different thing from the same wind blowing against the tidal-flow in shoal water. Before any coastal cruise, whatever the weather, the Coast

FIGURE 3

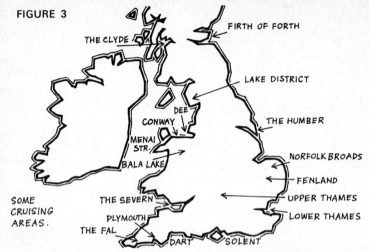

THE CLYDE

FIRTH OF FORTH

LAKE DISTRICT

DEE

CONWAY

THE HUMBER

MENAI STR.

BALA LAKE

NORFOLK BROADS

FENLAND

SOME CRUISING AREAS.

THE SEVERN

UPPER THAMES

PLYMOUTH

LOWER THAMES

THE FAL

DART

SOLENT

Guards should be informed. Two forms, *CG 66 A* and *B,* give them details on sail number, size, hull colour, E.T.D. and E.T.A. Always phone the Coast Guard before you leave harbour, and give any alterations or changes in plan. This will assist them as they pass your dinghy, from post to post, along the coast. They should always be telephoned on landing.

Several alternative plans should be worked out as you plan the passage, just in case the weather turns foul. Small boats have no place at sea on a lee shore or in winds much over Force-4. For offshore sailing, the dinghy should be carefully prepared, provisioned, and checked. Continuous maintenance on all moving gear should be carried out, while you are under way.

Offshore cruising, in dinghies, will never be a popular sport. However, if skipper and crew are experienced, and the cruise well prepared, a stable dinghy will be able to weather bad seas and make considerable ocean voyages. Several *Wayfarers,* my husband Frank's in particular, have travelled long distances, from the U.K. to Iceland, to Norway and to Poland, along the Mediterranean, along the Baltic, across the Channel and high into the Arctic, and across the Canadian Great Lakes. A Drascombe longboat has travelled from the U.K. to Australia and another cruised extensively in the Greek islands before sailing back to the U.K. These and other such cruises demand stamina, and skill from the crew, and a good well-found dinghy, but it proves that it is possible.

GOING FOREIGN

When 'going foreign' check that the boat insurance covers foreign waters. Also check car insurance. Dinghies like the *Mirror* can be car topped, others trailed, taken as deck cargo, or crated, and this greatly extends the choice of cruising grounds, but it's not cheap. When your floating home travels with you, pulling into foreign points adds a new dimension to a holiday abroad, and when you are more experienced, you can always sail over to the Continent, and save ferry costs!

SOCIAL SAILING

Social sailing will be catered for by the Cruising Secretary of your Class Association and also the Dinghy Cruising Association. Join both. Regular rallies are planned and you can sail together on the same stretch of water and, after the day's sail a beach party or pub evening means that an exchange of ideas on gear and boats is possible, and new friendships made. This often gets a newcomer confident enough to continue cruising, although many people, as they gain experience, being 'loners' at hearts, will prefer to travel alone.

PRE-PLANNING

Having found a spot, you then need to get out your tide tables and calculate high water for the day in question. Reeds Nautical Almanac contains tide tables for all parts of the coast, plus a host of other information, and is another indispensable aid to cruising. If the area is unknown to you, the more water you have the better. It is disappointing to discover that you cannot launch except two hours either side of high water, or some such snag, but it does happen, so be prepared for it. From the planned launch site and time, work back and plan your route and travel time. Remember your maximum towing speed will be 50 m.p.h. (see Chapter 7), and allow plenty of time to rig the boat and get organized, for putting to sea should never be rushed. If you intend camping, be sure it is permitted on the intended site or, if necessary, book a pitch.

To start with, don't be too ambitious. Try out the gear and crew in good conditions and on short cruises. Be prepared to learn slowly, and remember that a cautious seaman is not a coward.

Because local knowledge is always useful it is a good idea to pick an area and explore that thoroughly before you go elsewhere. Chichester harbour will give you a very good season's cruising, for example, and maybe next year you could try the East Coast. It saves petrol and buying masses of tidal flow charts as well!

The great thrill of dinghy cruising is going somewhere—and going anywhere in a dinghy is thrilling in itself.

Chapter 4

FITTINGS, EQUIPMENT & STOWAGE

Let us get two rules established. Firstly, all fittings, and every part of the craft must be strong enough to stand up to the rigours of a cruise in *rough weather*. Secondly, however sound you *believe* your craft and equipment to be, you must check and inspect it EVERY TIME before you put to sea. As a pilot inspects his aircraft before every take-off, so you must inspect your craft before every cruise. Quite often you'll spot something that will make you thankful for the precaution.

A strong, well-maintained boat is the best insurance. Screw fittings should be ·through-bolted, and of stainless steel, or galvanized. Brass screws should be avoided as they de-zinc in contact with salt water. Replace all running rigging at the first sign of fraying. Floorboards and decking should be treated with a non-slip substance. Check the centreboard pivot and bush it if it leaks. Check all drainage bungs as well, and carry spares.

When buying fittings, buy the heavy-duty type. Light, natty fittings have no place in a cruising boat.

BUOYANCY COMPARTMENTS

As these have a safety as well as a stowage function, check them regularly. Be sure the seals are complete, and the clips secure.

Buoyancy bags can be lashed under the side benches. We have heavy duty bags, which we also use, to roll the dinghy up the beach, and as fenders in harbour or when alongside other craft. Using inflatable boat rollers like these, a two-man crew can manhandle a loaded dinghy up a soft beach with ease. This brings me to another useful rule: 'WHENEVER POSSIBLE EVERYTHING SHOULD HAVE AT LEAST TWO USES'.

ALTERNATIVE PROPULSION

If there is no wind, you'll need oars, paddles, a tow rope or an outboard. Therefore you will also need rowlocks, and an engine bracket. Galvanized rowlocks are better than plastic ones. The oars must have leathers on them, and be as long as possible. The length is governed by the stowage space aboard. The straight blade is better than the spoon type, for you can use them to plumb the depths inshore (another double use). Protect the ends with glass-fibre tape. An oar lashed along one of the side benches widens the bench enough for someone to sleep on it. Some friends of ours sleep four adults comfortably on a *Wayfarer* like that. So that's a third use.

SCULLING

A socket on the transom for a sculling rowlock can be useful, but it must be positioned so that the rowlock does not impede the tiller. Sculling is a useful and attractive small boat skill, and one you should learn.

You don't usually need the rudder while sculling.

ENGINES

A dinghy transom is not usually designed for the weight of an engine, and many dinghies do not function well under power. Nevertheless, there are occasions when a light outboard, like one of the robust *Seagull* range, can be useful. Remember though, that an engine is *useless,* indeed *dangerous,* if it won't start when you want it. They need regular maintenance, pose stowage problems—especially as they can affect the compass; and are an attraction to thieves. They are not cheap, so if you buy one, ask your boat manufacturer which sort he recommends. Don't ask the engine manufacturer. Be sure you know simple engine maintenance, and carry oars as well.

ANCHORS

No dinghy should put to sea without at least one anchor, and preferably two. They should be lashed securely into the boat with shock-cords, or they may move and damage the hull, but they must be instantly available, in case of need.

Anchors hold better if about two fathoms (say 4 metres) of 3/16ths to 5/16ths galvanized chain is shackled to it. The anchor

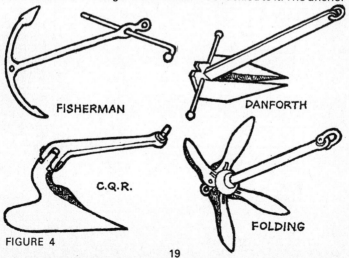

FISHERMAN   DANFORTH

C.Q.R.   FOLDING

FIGURE 4

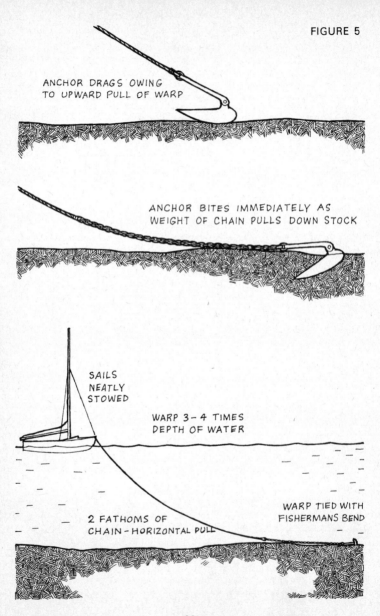

FIGURE 5

ANCHOR DRAGS OWING
TO UPWARD PULL OF WARP

ANCHOR BITES IMMEDIATELY AS
WEIGHT OF CHAIN PULLS DOWN STOCK

SAILS
NEATLY
STOWED

WARP 3-4 TIMES
DEPTH OF WATER

WARP TIED WITH
FISHERMANS BEND

2 FATHOMS OF
CHAIN-HORIZONTAL PULL

warp should be fastened to the chain with a fisherman's bend, and you need plenty of line. You need 30 metres or more of warp for each anchor, in terylene of 7/8ths'' circumference. The warps need to be coiled down into the craft and secured. A 7lb. anchor, with adequate warps and chain should be right for the average cruising dinghy. Always err on the heavy side for all your gear.

There are, basically, four types of dinghy anchor.

1. Folding: easily stowed, but drags rather easily.
2. Danforth: easily stowed, with good holding capability.
3. C.Q.R. (Plough): awkward to stow, good holding.
4. Fisherman's: good on rocky ground, but can foul its warp.

SPARE RUDDER AND TILLER
The R.Y.A. insist on their cruising courses that a spare rudder and tiller are carried. If you have room this is certainly a sound principle. If not, you must check your steering gear carefully before you go, and be able to carry out repairs, if anything gets damaged. You can use an oar to replace the rudder, and even use floor boards as temporary lee boards, in emergencies.

BAILERS
A large sponge, and a bucket, secured inboard with a lanyard, should always be carried. In addition, some people have Elvestrom type bailers fitted, which are very efficient if the boat is sailing fast enough.

Nowadays in 'Wanderer' we always have a flexible hose hand-pump fitted by the centreboard case, and the helmsman can do a bit of pumping if required, while still steering the boat, although it is usually the crew's job.

BOAT SPARES
You need plenty of spares, and I suggest that, as a minimum you carry: spare gooseneck; split-pins; shackles; bungs; lengths of wire; terylene line; pintle and gudgeon; screws, spare plywood (for a wooden boat); deflated buoyancy bags.

BOSUN'S STORES
These should consist of all tools and materials necessary to carry out any repair job afloat. You need: an adjustable spanner; combination pliers; screw drivers; a good knife; shackle key; a small hack-saw with spare blades; patches of sail cloth; terylene thread and needles; oil; grease; waterproof glue; oilskin mending

patches; blocks; torch and torch batteries; whistle; fog horn; lantern spares, lifelines and bulbs.

Yes, it's a lot isn't it! But we've found it all necessary.

NAVIGATION AIDS

You need a compass, charts, dividers, tidal stream atlas and a tide table guide, like Reeds Almanac. Port guides are also useful. Keep these dry. We'll talk about their use in Chapter 8.

COMPASS ERROR

The compass must be positioned where the helmsman can see it from any position and where the deviation from metal fittings and stores is reduced to the minimum. You must know the deviation caused by all the usual fittings. We'll come back to this later, but for now just be aware of the danger.

LIGHTS

All cruising dinghies *should* be fitted with the accepted green (starboard) and red (port) lights, plus a white masthead light, although these are not at present compulsory for most dinghies. (In practice you are usually ashore by dusk). Depending on your craft you had better check out the lighting requirements.

If you are anchored offshore, a lantern hoisted to the masthead can serve as a riding light. A torch shone on the sails will indicate your position to another boat, if you are making a short sail at night.

SAFETY EQUIPMENT

Check all buoyancy, of course. Lifelines should be worn at all times, and are frequently more practical than lifejackets, when working under sail. You should wear a lifejacket or buoyancy aid as well, in any sort of weather. Never skimp on safety equipment. You should also carry a First Aid kit and know how to use it.

FLARES

Six white and six red flares will be sufficient. Buy the large size rather than the mini-flares. Read the instructions carefully so that you know when, where, and how to use them. Hold them in a gloved hand, away from the face, and don't fire into the sail. Replace your flares regularly, and never use them except in real emergency.

STOWAGE

We haven't yet covered all the personal gear, food, sleeping, cooking and tent equipment, but let's talk about stowage. The

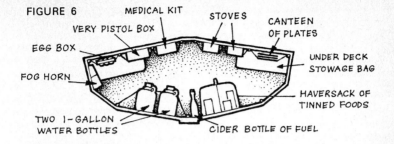

FIGURE 6

amount of gear you have to stow will horrify you but there are a few rules which will prove helpful.

1. All gear must be tied and shock-corded into the boat. Nothing must be loose.

2. Spread the weight evenly fore and aft, with the heavy gear in the centre, or sailing performance will be affected.

3. Keep all metal items, engine, tins, bosun's stores etc., as far away as possible from the compass.

4. Stow all clothing and sleeping gear in sealed plastic bags, in a buoyancy compartment, or tied up under the side benches out of any water washing about on the floorboards.

5. Be wary of all fuel and flares. Fuel is a hazard at sea, and wet flares are useless.

6. Work out where is best, then stow everything in the SAME PLACE ON EVERY TRIP. Then you can spot if anything is missing from its usual place. Try and keep the cockpit uncluttered.

All this sounds like a lot of expensive gear, and it certainly isn't cheap, but you don't need it all at once. You can cruise quite happily with your basic boat, adding more gear as you get more adventurous. Just have it when you need it, that's all.

PRACTISE STOWAGE

However much gear this seems, it's going to look a lot more piled up beside the dinghy, so practise stowing it in the boat on land a few times first. You will find there are all sorts of ways for saving space and having stuff to hand when you need it. Once you have established the best place for a particular piece of gear, always stow it there. Then if it's not there you know you've forgotten it.

Chapter 5

LIVING ABOARD—CAMPING ASHORE

We now have to look at the other items of gear you will need to live, eat and sleep in a small boat, or while camping ashore. Here again, you probably have a lot of it anyway, or can borrow it for occasional use.

CLOTHING

The first point, on clothing, is that 'natty-yachting' gear is not necessary. You need to keep warm and if possible, dry. A wet-suit is fine, but soft wool sweaters and trousers retain body heat and are comfortable on long watches. Sitting still over long periods causes the body to lose heat steadily, so protection for the head and hands is essential, as is something to pad the rear! Oilskins keep you dry, and more important, keep the wind at bay. Have a full set and the top must have a hood. Woollen underclothes should be worn, and a spare set of clothing carried to change into if you get wet. Wear gym-shoes, yachting shoes, or boots (the latter two sizes too large for easy removal). Wear two pairs of socks.

FOOD

Eat regularly. Always have a good meal before you sail, as you may not feel like one later on! A lot of food can and should be prepared ashore. Flasks of soup, hot drinks, and stews, can be cooked ashore and eaten at sea. Eat from an insulated bowl or mug. This keeps the food hot and won't burn your lips. Tupperware containers are ideal, but glass containers should be left at home.

Apart from considerations of convenience, you can eat anything you like. Convenience foods are a boon to all dinghy cruising people and campers. Don't forget to take a tin opener, and *WATER*. You'll need about a litre per person per day, and more if you love lots of tea!

To calculate how much food you need, prepare a meal chart showing how many eggs, bacon rashers, cups of tea or whatever, you and the crew will eat at each meal, multiply the items by the number of days and meals, and, behold, you have a shopping list.

COOKERS

Cookers are not usually lit until one is at anchor, or ashore. Cooking afloat, keep a wary eye open for the passing power-boat, or unexpected wave. Camping-gaz or Optimus stoves are good makes, and a small gas stove or cooker can be fixed in gimbals to a thwart or side bench. A windshield on the stove is important, to get the maximum benefit from the flame, as there always seems to be a breeze at mealtimes. An asbestos blanket over pot and stove is a good idea. Remember if using solid fuel or gas, that you need spare fuel canisters.

Be very careful of fuels and gas vapour. This can settle in the bilges, and be ignited by that post-meal cigarette. Fuel should be kept in a metal container marked PETROL or PARAFFIN.

COOKING GEAR
Buy a good aluminium cook-set, from any camping shop. Plastic collapsible containers from any camping shop are ideal for fresh water. Knives, forks, spoons, mug, plastic spatula, salt, pepper, tin opener, corkscrew, bottle opener, matches and lighter, scouring pad, and J-cloths. This will enable you to cook and clean up afterwards, and remember that sand is excellent for scouring pots and plates.

SLEEPING BAGS
Bags filled with man-made fibre are preferable—and cheaper— than bags made of down. Man-made fibre fillings retain their insulation properties when wet. Since you will be lying in close proximity to the water it seems sensible to buy gear which is least likely to be affected by the inevitable damp. Stow the bag in a double plastic bag, and keep it in one of the sealed compartments, or lashed up with shock-cord under the side benches.

AIRBEDS OR SLEEPING MATS
Which you choose is a matter of personal choice, but a mat takes up less room than an airbed, if you sleep aboard, and is just as comfortable ashore. I would recommend a mat; the Karrimat or Adsmat being popular makes.

DINGHY BIVOUAC
If you have a groundsheet to keep the rain and spray off, you won't need a tent if you sleep aboard. You can attach the main halyard to the boom, to make a topping lift, hoist the boom to make a ridge, and drape the sail over it to make a serviceable shelter. Sailors are supposed to use their initiative!

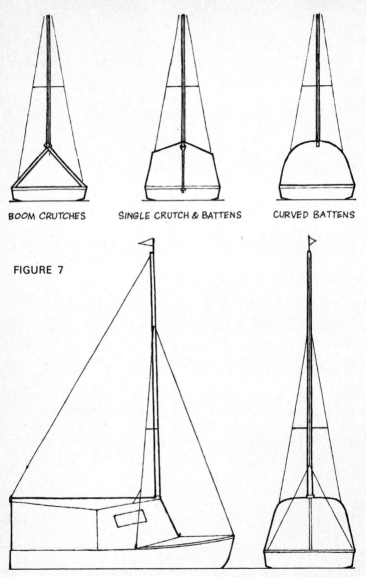

BOOM CRUTCHES SINGLE CRUTCH & BATTENS CURVED BATTENS

FIGURE 7

WAYFARER TENT COVER

BOAT TENT

A water-tight, weather-proofed, low-windage *boat tent* turns a sailing dinghy into a home. Inside, you can be more cozy, and have more headroom than many keel boat cabins allow. Tent materials can be man-made, such as terylene, or. nylon, which is cheaper and rot and shrink-proof, or natural materials such as canvas, or treble-proofed Egyptian cotton, which is expensive, will shrink and rot, but has fewer condensation problems, and is easier to stitch and repair. On weight, 10 ozs. man-made fibres as against 12 ozs. natural fibres for tents, mean that the nylon tent is a slightly lighter bundle to pack. New materials are constantly being advertized, all trying to combine the best qualities of both natural *and* man-made materials, so you need to read the magazines and see what is available.

TENT SHAPE

The shape of the boat tent is an individual thing, but windage must not be excessive or you will spend your time at anchor busily sailing back and forth around your mooring!

The Cruising members of the Wayfarer Association have done some research into tent designs. The basic one is a ridge type. The material is slung over the boom which is positioned at a pre-set height by the gooseneck and the main halyard providing a topping lift arrangement to the boom. Crutches on the transom hold the boom firm. Openings to the tent can be made at the bows or shrouds and they can be sealed by velcro strips, nylon zips or lacings. A tight sleeve of material ensures that no rain drips down the mast and the shrouds. The tent can be fixed to the hull by velcro strips sewn to the bottom of the tent, and glued to the underside of the rubbing strakes, and washboards. Sometimes, as an alternative, a bolt rope is sewn along the tent bottom and for final tensioning the gooseneck is lifted up the mast to make a snug fit and raise the tent height.

Alternative shapes, giving more headroom, are largely a matter of using extra supports. A tunnel-shaped tent can be made over circular battens or curved curtain rails, and an even more elegant tent can be made by sliding bamboo, or light alloy rods into pockets in the tent corners, securing them to the shrouds, and thus giving a wall to the tent. Careful adjustments of height and angles between walls and roof, mean that rainwater does not sit in the awnings. The sides of this tent can be rolled up to make a sun-shade or windshield.

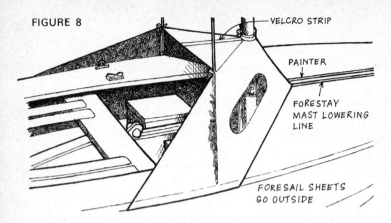

FIGURE 8

VELCRO STRIP

PAINTER

FORESTAY
MAST LOWERING
LINE

FORESAIL SHEETS
GO OUTSIDE

SPRAYHOODS

Even on a dinghy, a sprayhood can be useful. Beneath them, gear or children gain protection from wind and spray, and provided it is not too high, movement of the boom and kicking strap is not impeded when the spray hood is in position. Transparent plastic windows can be sewn into it, as indeed they can be sewn into the sides and roofs of the boat tent.

SLEEPING ASHORE

If you intend to beach the boat and sleep ashore as many do, be sure you have permission to camp. Everywhere belongs to somebody, and if you camp without permission you can be ordered off. There are many camp guides published each year, and magazines such as *'Camping'* and *'Practical Camper'* all publish regular information on new sites.

You need a light ridge-tent, with a fitted groundsheet to keep the sand out, and a porched flysheet. The flysheet will cut down condensation, and you can cook in the shelter of the porch. Take a range of tent pegs with you which will enable you to cope with soft, sandy, or rocky ground. Nylon tents are light and strong, and available at a range of prices. See the selection at any outdoor shop.

If possible, bring the dinghy ashore, on the inflatable rollers, to well above the high tide mark, but put an anchor out anyway, just in case. If you leave it afloat, float it off into deeper water, and anchor it so that it comes to no harm during the hours of darkness when the tides change. See Page 56 for some hints on anchoring from the beach. Don't leave valuables aboard.

Chapter 6

WEATHER FORECASTS

There are lots of books that can tell you all about forecasting, but I must include some mention here to impress upon you that dinghy cruising is completely dominated by the weather. It would be a very imprudent sailor indeed who put out in bad conditions, or stayed out if he could get to shelter. Winds over Force-4 are to be avoided but my great fear is not wind, but FOG.

FOG
This is the most frightening weather condition, for the small boat sailor. If you encounter it while on a cruise, the drill is to anchor in shallow water, out of the shipping lanes and away from main channel. Get ashore if you possibly can.

GALES
Dinghy cruising in heavy weather (over Force-6) is best avoided, but if you are caught out, you must, as the wind gets up, take early precautions and prepare for worsening conditions by putting on life-jackets and life-lines (if not already worn), securing all stores and hatches, and taking in sail. The cruising sailor must *reef for the gusts.* Dinghies will survive the most severe gales given an experienced crew, and plenty of searoom, but I wouldn't recommend staying out, or being bold, in the face of bad weather. Stay ashore or run for shelter.

It follows therefore, that the dinghy cruising sailor must have a very good grasp of weather lore, forecasting, and be able to assess very accurately, the development of weather patterns during the cruise.

FORECAST SOURCES
Radio: Never miss the chance to hear a broadcast forecast, and always know the times at which they are transmitted, for radio forecasts are accurate and regularly updated. Gale warnings precede each shipping forecast. See the Radio Times and local press for broadcast times as they are, unfortunately, subject to change from time to time.
Local Radio: There are a growing number of local radio stations situated in cruising areas. Radio Solent and Radio Medway are two examples. These broadcast forecasts, and local gale warnings for yachtsmen. Again see the local press for wavelength details and broadcast times.

FIGURE 9

FAEROES

BAILEY

VIKING

FAIR ISLE

SKULE SKERRY○

HEBRIDES

MINCHES

WICK○

CROMARTY

FORTIES

FISHER

ROCKALL

TIREE○

MALIN

FORTH

BELL ROCK○

MALIN HEAD○

PRESTWICK○

TYNE

DOGGER

GERMAN BIGHT

RONALDSWAY○

IRISH SEA

HUMBER

DOWSING○

SHANNON

VALENTIA○

FASTNET

LUNDY

THAMES

GALLOPER○

DOVER

VARNE○

ROYAL SOVEREIGN○

PORTLAND BILL○

WIGHT

SCILLY○

PORTLAND

SOLE

PLYMOUTH

SEA AREAS AND COASTAL STATIONS

FINISTERRE

BISCAY

30

Obviously you need a radio set to pick up the forecasts. A transistor set will usually do as reception over the water is very good, but be sure it has the right wavebands. Some foreign sets do not have an adequate Medium band, and others cannot pick up Radio 4. *Don't miss long wave shipping forecasts.* We carry a D.F. (Direction Finding) set under the foredeck, clipping the aerial to the shrouds when in use, which gives better reception. It's expensive, but will last us for years. Keep any radio, and the batteries, well wrapped against the inevitable damp and corrosion.

T.V.: T.V. forecasts are excellent, since the forecaster gives an explanatory chat, and makes predictions for 48 hours ahead. The dinghy sailor wants to know the *future,* not just what is happening now, but what is likely to happen in the days ahead, but of course, there is not a great deal of local information.

Press: The 'quality' papers, like the *'Times', 'Telegraph',* and *'Guardian'* give the best forecasts, with weather maps showing the coastline, but all press forecasts, because of distribution delays, tend to be a bit out of date.

Local Weather Stations: The telephone numbers of the local stations can be found in the telephone directory. Some have a taped forecast (like the speaking clock) but in others you can speak to an operator. Always ring the local station for a forecast before setting sail. Tell them where you are going, for there are often variations to the weather conditions caused by physical features, which they know about and you may not. NEVER NEGLECT TO GET THIS INFORMATION.

WEATHER ELEMENTS AND TERMS

For even a rudimentary knowledge of weather forecasting to be of use, you must understand the jargon:—

PRESSURE

Pressure is measured in *bars*—and the instrument which measures pressure is called a barometer. In meteorological circles the bar is divided into millibars (mb) and the normal air pressure at *sea-level* is 1013 millibars. Pressure varies, and rises and falls in the pressure, from about the 1000 mb. mark, are very good pointers to the weather, for the limits of pressure usually lie between 950 mb. and 1050 mb. As a *general* rule falling pressure indicates the approach of bad weather, while rising pressure indicates good weather, but a quick rise in pressure usually falls again, indicating the approach of more bad weather. Official weather forecasts give barometric pressure in millibars.

On a weather map, points of equal pressure are joined up by lines called *isobars.*

HUMIDITY

The atmosphere always contains a certain amount of water vapour, and when this vapour condenses we get different types of weather; especially fog, rain, snow, or the most obvious example, cloud.

The air can only hold just so much water vapour in any form, and when this maximum point is reached the air is said to be saturated.

Humidity is expressed in percentages, for example, say 75°F with 80% humidity, which would be sticky. As the temperature falls, the air cools, and it can cool until condensation results. This point, the point at which condensation occurs, is called the *dew point,* and this means, as stated above, the possibility of fog, or the formation of clouds.

Remember that cold air holds less water than warm air and that cold air tends to sink, for these facts are relevant to a lot of weather phenomena.

WIND

If we hark back to pressure, note first that wind is usually heading from where pressure is high to where pressure is low, trying as it were, to fill up the difference. Owing to the rotation of the earth, air currents or winds are usually skewed off their direct course, thereby producing those whorls on the weather maps which show wind direction.

Wind is described in two ways: speed and direction.

Wind speed is expressed in miles per hour, knots (sea miles per hour) or the graduations of the Beaufort Scale. Wind force is measured with an instrument called an anenometer, and remember, wind direction refers to the direction the wind is coming FROM not going TO. Wind temperatures vary according to their direction, the time of year, and the surface they pass over.

In the U.K. south and westerly winds are wet and relatively warm, for they pick up moisture crossing the Atlantic, and the sea in winter tends to be warmer than the land. Because these winds are warmer they can hold more moisture and bring cloudy weather and prolonged periods of rain. Conversely, northern and easterly winds tend to be dry and very cold. In summer, the easterly winds can be warmer, for in summer the land warms up more quickly than the sea, and the winds pick up heat while blowing over it. High altitude winds can be quite different from winds at sea level.

FRONTS

A 'front' is the frontier line between an area of warm air and an area of cold air, or vice-versa, and marks the edges of two air masses of different origin. The cold air will fall, and the warm air will rise over the cold air, condensing as it does so into clouds and rain.

In a 'warm front' the air temperature changes from cold to warm as the warm front passes through, while in a 'cold front' the reverse happens, the air changes from warm to cold.

'HIGHS' AND 'LOWS', OCCLUSIONS

In an anti-cyclone, or 'high', the pressure is high, the winds light, and the weather *generally* fine and warm. Anti-cyclones are slow moving, and you can, incidentally, get a cloudy anti-cyclone. They don't always mean fine weather. You can also get depressions or 'lows' when the pressure falls and the weather usually deteriorates.

You can experience a 'ridge of high pressure' between two 'lows', in which for a brief period, perhaps a few hours, perhaps a day or two, the skies clear, the winds drop, and the sun comes out. Then the 'ridge' passes and the clouds come in again. When two weather patterns mix and merge, you get what is known as an occlusion, a mixture of unsettled weather.

Away from the centre of a 'high' the winds increase. An anti-cyclone centred over, say, the Azores, can mean fine summer weather for England, but with high, force 4-6 winds. So remember to note the centre of the 'high' when making your weather calculations. For all these, the barometer and your eyes are the best warning.

FORECAST TERMS

Let's look at these in more detail and define what the radio forcaster means when he uses words like 'soon', 'gale', or 'imminent'.

Imminent: Within 6 hours of warning
Soon: Within 6 to 12 hours of warning
Later: After 12 hours of warning

GALE FORCE

Gale: Wind 34 knots or more, or a wind with 43 knots gusts.

Severe Gale: Wind 41 knots or more, or a wind with 52 knots gusts.

Storm: Wind 48 knots or more, or a wind with gusts up to 61 knots.

33

VISIBILITY

Good	More than five nautical miles
Moderate	Two to five nautical miles
Poor	1,100 yards to two nautical miles
Fog	Less than 1,100 yards.

BACKING AND VEERING

Winds do not just change direction, they 'back' or 'veer'. When winds *back*, they go in an anti-clockwise direction, and when they *veer* they go clockwise. A 'backing' wind usually increases in strength, while 'veering' winds often drop, although there may be squalls.

SQUALLS

A line squall is occasionally encountered when sailing. This is a very well marked cold front, usually appearing from the North-West as a line of low black clouds. As it passes strong squalls of wind, often with heavy rain and thunder can be expected, and then the usual post-cold front sequence of events will follow. It is best to take in sail, until you see just what is going to happen.

CLOUDS

Because frontal weather systems are associated with air masses, clouds form as the result of the presence and accumulation of water vapour in the atmosphere. Some clouds are formed by convection, but most are caused by the dynamic effect of fronts. Learn all you can about clouds.

Since certain cloud types are associated with approaching frontal pressure systems, the yachtsman, if he can identify cloud types, can see approaching weather.

Space is not available here to illustrate all the clouds, but we can discuss the way in which clouds are described.

Clouds are classified by their heights and shape.

	Height	
High	18,000 feet plus	CIRRUS
Medium	8,000 to 18,000 feet	ALTO
Low	up to 8000 feet	STRATUS

Cirrus, high shredded cloud, usually indicates wind, and all sailors know what a 'mackerel sky' (Alto-stratus) means. *"Mackerel sky and mares' tails, make tall ships carry small sails."*

The next definition is by shape, and this again falls into three main types:

Feather type	CIRROFORM
Layer type	STRATIFORM
Heap type	CUMULIFORM

Most sailors will have the time while afloat, to watch the formation of cloud patterns, and I urge you to learn all you can about them.

LOCAL KNOWLEDGE
Never pass up the chance for a chat with local people, fishermen, coast guard or fellow yachtsmen. They can give you advice about local hazards and danger spots in local waters. If it isn't offered, ask for it.

MAKE YOUR OWN FORECAST
If you are going on a weekend cruise you must start gathering weather information at least two days before i.e., on the Wednesday. You need to obtain weather information in the days before the trip, so that you can see what sort of weather is building up.

There is a great deal to learn about the weather, and you can never know too much. I hope this brief chapter has at least impressed upon you the necessity for obtaining complete and regular weather information, and given you the taste for more knowledge.

For a fuller understanding may I recommend the *'Spur Book of Weather Lore'* also published in this series.

Chapter 7

TRAILING, LAUNCHING, RECOVERY

Trailing is an essential part of dinghy cruising, a thought that only strikes people when it is pointed out! Given a car, a trailer, a motorway (and a dinghy) you can cruise anywhere.

There are unfortunately, a few snags, and in this present age, a growing list of rules and regulations. Since you don't want to be stopped by the Police—which is hardly the happiest note to start the trip on—let's look at the regulations first.

WEIGHT AND LENGTH REGULATIONS

The overall length of boat and trailer must not exceed 23' (7 metres). The maximum permitted width is 7' 6" (2.3 metres), unless the towing vehicle weighs more than 2 tons. Any trailer over 7 metres must have four wheels with the trailer's wheelbase not less than 3/5ths of the overall length. Trailers with an *unladen* weight (without the boat) of less than 2 cwt., do not need to have brakes, but heavier trailers must have them. Complicated isn't it!

SPEED

Contrary to popular belief the maximum permitted speed is 40 m.p.h. but you can go up to 50 m.p.h. if you follow certain rules, i.e., *Kerbside Weight:* This is the part that affects 90% of dinghy owners. So read this carefully. A trailer *without brakes* must not weigh more than 60% of the 'kerbside weight' of the car. The 'kerbside weight' is the all-up weight of the car, without passengers. You can find this weight by going to the local weighbridge or by ringing your garage and trailer supplier, finding the weights and doing a simple sum.

Marking: Once you have ascertained the 'kerbside weight' you must show it on the car. A typewritten strip stuck on the windscreen above the licence disc will deflate the most gleeful copper! Otherwise paint it neatly on a nearside chassis member. Similarly, on the trailer you mark the trailer weight on the external nearside so that both car and trailer carry a note of their weight.

Lastly, a plate with '50' must be fixed on the trailer, facing the rear, and ours is fixed to the number plate.

LIGHTS AND SPEED LIMIT

You must carry a light board on the trailer, with the car number, rear, stop and direction indicating lights. The number plate must be of a reflecting material.

PROJECTING LOADS (ENGINES)
The rules here are specific to the inch!

	Projections		**Marking**
Front & Rear projection	0-3'6" (1.07m.)	=	No marking.
3'6" to 6'0" (1.83 m.)		=	Some clear marking i.e., a red flag.
6'0" and over		=	A marker warning triangle must be carried.

The general rule is that all projections are a danger and must be marked or covered. Outboard propellers are certainly a risk and must be masked.

There is a rule covering all this—'Regulation 90'—which states that apart from conforming to these specific requirements, all towing and trailing gear must be suitable for the task, and in good condition. So you should keep the trailer looking good, as well as in tip-top order mechanically.

Galvanized or painted trailers and trolleys, if well maintained should last many years, but be sure they conform to the regulations.

When towing, low speeds should be observed, and sudden acceleration avoided. Check that there is no chafe, and that the ropes or webbing are in position. These checks should be made during stops on the journey. When towing, remember never to take bends sharply and allow ample time for braking. When the journey is over—remember to loosen the securing ropes across the dinghy and holding the bows down. Never leave this job until launching the following day as this puts unfair strain in the hull of the dinghy.

This really does seem a great number of rules, but if you take them one at a time they should not prove too daunting.

TRAILER MAINTENANCE
Road trailers, these days, cost a great deal of money, and they repay any care lavished on them. Sea water is not the best treatment for hot wheels which have travelled many miles, especially if the bearings are unsealed. After immersion, they may need to be pumped full of grease again, while rinsing the trailer with fresh water after salt water launching is a good idea. Most

road trailers have adjustable chocks to support the boat bilges, and these should be adjusted to the individual boat hull, while some modern road trailers have glass fibre moulded cradles, and for long journeys, the moulded shape is better for the dinghy.

A spare trailer wheel is really essential, as a puncture to a trailer tyre could immobilise you miles from anywhere.

Rollers, wheel bearings and brakes, all need constant attention and lubricating with grease or oil, as salt water is not good for them.

Once on the trailer, the dinghy must be padded well and tied down securely. Chafe must be guarded against, and therefore rudder, tiller spars and all loose parts of the equipment packed carefully. Really heavy gear should not be trailed in the dinghy.

TROLLEYS

A launching trolley does not usually have wheel bearings, so the axle with solid hubs rotating on it merely needs the odd dab of grease. A trolley, as well as a trailer, is the ideal, as using the trolley keeps the trailer out of the water. It pays to use a trolley except when the dinghy is travelling along the roads.

For launching, the large trolley wheels and wide tyres ensure the boat will not get bogged down on the soft ground. Search for a slipway or gently sloping beach. The trolley should be run stern first into the water, the dinghy gently floated off, and the trolley removed to some safe place, for security, and to avoid obstructing other people launching.

Most commercial trailers and trolleys are too high for easy launching and recovery.

BEACH ROLLERS

We also carry tough, heavy-duty buoyancy bags which we use to roll our *Wayfarer* up the beach, above the high-tide mark. With practice this becomes very easy and has got us ashore snugly in some lonely spots. On barnacled rocks, though, they can puncture, so you need to add a puncture repair outfit to your bosun's stores.

Placing boat rollers under the dinghy until she will literally roll up the beach makes really light work of rolling the boat on land or at times when a trolley is not available. It is better to load a dinghy before launching—otherwise the crew can have the unpleasant job of holding the boat off a pebble beach, knee deep in water, while the loading is done afloat, with the risk of dropping something in the water. It is a good plan to come ashore as soon as possible after high water, as this means less work handling the

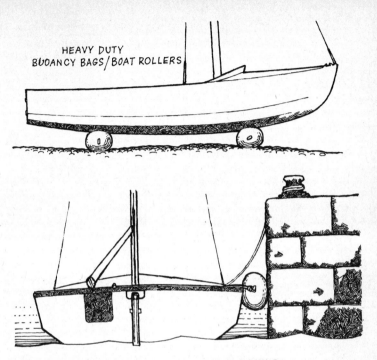

HEAVY DUTY
BUOANCY BAGS/BOAT ROLLERS

BOAT ROLLERS USED AS FENDERS

FIGURE 10

boat ashore and also a longer sleep since the high water will float one off the beach roughly 12½ hours later.

RECOVERY

A loaded dinghy is often difficult to launch, but it is usually far harder to recover, and for a heavy boat a good trailer/trolley combination becomes a necessity. One fitted with a winch is now available, but as with most other things, you get what you pay for, and they are not cheap. Docking arms fitted to the trolley or trailer mean that the dinghy can be floated into position on the trailer.

A stern eyebolt through-bolted low down on the bows of the dinghy means that one can haul a dinghy up difficult slopes and beaches if all else fails.

Using a three part block and pulley, we can haul our heavy *Wayfarer* up river banks, using nearby trees to secure the pulley.

Great care must be taken, with enough manpower available, in recovery of a heavily ladened cruising dinghy. The heaviest stores should be off-loaded before the dinghy is pulled on to the trolley or road trailer. Sometimes a rope can be put around the tow bar of the car and this can help to draw the dinghy out of the water. The tow rope must be tied low around a firm part of the trolley, and then very slow *controlled* speeds will ensure the dinghy is not jumped off.

SECURING THE DINGHY ON THE TRAILER

Nylon webbing or ropes should tie the dinghy on to the trailer and the bows and mast must also be tied down and checked before a road journey is started. Padding takes time, but the varnish appreciates it. If the dinghy is to be left in the dinghy park on the trailer or trolley, the wheels should be chocked with stones or blocks, and the boat tied down. It goes without saying that after a salt water sail, the sails, boat, and oilskins will benefit from a wash down in fresh water. If the dinghy is stored propped up, rain water will run off the cover and out of the bilges, if the bungs are left out. Never let the dinghy fill with rainwater in the dinghy park.

LAUNCHING

If you have to launch the dinghy from a road trailer it is sensible to tip up the trailer, and slide the dinghy off the chocks. Stones or blocks put behind the wheels will stop the trailer sliding towards the water and so immersing the wheel bearings. It is important to keep the dinghy central on the chocks, holding the painter to ensure the dinghy does not enter the water in an uncontrollable rush. Before launching, somebody should walk over the area and check there are no submerged rocks or stakes which could damage the dinghy. The centreboard should be secured up with the pin through it before launching, and the rudder should not normally be fitted until the dinghy is afloat. Elvstrom bailers should be closed before launching and bungs checked. The dinghy hull is most vulnerable when it does not have the support of the water on all sides, so only in real emergencies should anybody climb into the dinghy when it is on the trailer.

Chapter 8

NAVIGATION AND PILOTAGE

The racing helm get along quite nicely for years without much knowledge of navigation, but the dinghy cruising helm needs to have at least a basic grasp of all the essentials.

Fortunately they are well covered in a companion volume *Chart and Compass* by Ted Broadhurst (Spur Book Venture Guide—90p), and I just want to run over the basics here.

NAVIGATION EQUIPMENT

You need a set of navigation aids and the following are essential.

1. A good marine compass.
2. Charts of the sea area, either Admiralty, Stanfords, or Imrays. Stick to one make.
3. Reeds Nautical Almanac (An annual publication).
4. Tidal flow charts.
5. Dividers.
6. Parallel rules or Douglas Protractors.
7. Several hexagonal shaped 2B pencils.
8. A soft rubber.
9. A reliable watch.
10. A waterproof sleeve.

With this equipment, some instruction and a little practice, you will soon be able to make short passages across estuaries and along the coast with a good degree of accuracy.

In dinghy cruising, navigation must, as far as possible, be done before the cruise begins. Spread out the charts and study them carefully, memorizing anchorages, hazards and alternative shelters, shallows, tide rips and much other valuable information in the comfort of home. When under sail, the chart can be folded to the area required and protected in a chart case or plastic sheet. Notes can be made on it with a chinagraph pencil.

In a dinghy, navigation is much more of an art than a science. The principles are straightforward, but the enormous variation caused by wind, tide and weather, render their application an art which only experience can teach. The novice tends to have a passive approach, merely marking his place on the chart with a neat cross, which fixes the boat's position. The experienced navigator has a more positive and far-sighted approach; after fixing his position, he will recognise that overfalls, tide rips and other dangers, need to be taken into account. He will also recognise that his dead reckoning position is only based on calculated guesswork.

CHARTS

Charts are indispensable. Without them the sailor cannot fix his position. He will have little or no idea of the bottom, or the depth in which he is sailing, nor can he lay off a course to avoid danger or pick up any point out of sight.

The chart is a graphical representation of the land he is passing (if any) and the sea-bed over which he is sailing. There are three main chart 'brands': Admiralty; Stanfords; and Imrays.

Stanfords are very good for dinghy sailors as they are clearly coloured and give courses from one harbour to another. Imrays are also good, while many people swear by Admiralty charts, which are really excellent.

Whichever one you choose, stick to it. That way you learn the symbols they employ and can read them quickly.

Admiralty chart No. 5011 which is more like a book, shows the symbols used to indicate features at sea or on the coast, and all Admiralty charts give fantastic detail. Buy a 5011 and study the symbols until you can 'read' a chart. They are accurate down to the last rock! On one occasion we were cruising in Norway and the chart showed a little cove with a single farm marked, *'Seljistokken'.* The farmer invited us home for a meal, and as we were leaving I asked him his name. He replied that his *name* was Seljistokken!

Projections on these charts are either Mercator or gnomonic. The Mercator's projection is most useful to yachtsmen, for on this projection a course laid off between two points will appear as a straight line and it is possible to read off the course directly on the "compass rose." Over great distances this projection becomes distorted as the lines of longitude have to be shown as parallels instead of converging towards the poles, but that need not concern us here. For measuring distance, use the latitude scale at the side of the chart. One minute of latitude = 1 nautical mile. Measure off the pencil line with the dividers, and transfer the dividers to the side of the chart where you can read off the distance.

On each chart will be found at least one 'compass rose'. The outer ring gives true bearings and the inner rose is the magnetic one. In the U.K. magnetic variation is decreasing a few minutes annually, and to convert the chart bearings from true to magnetic,

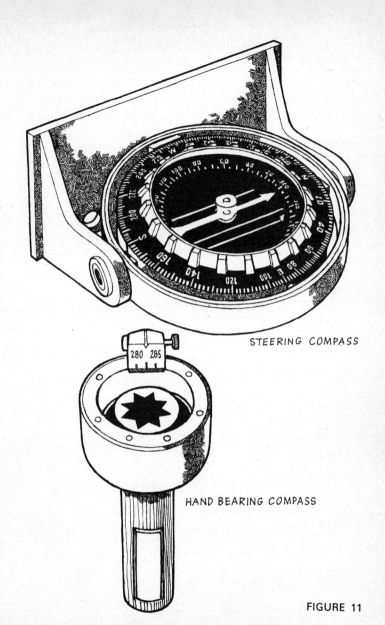

STEERING COMPASS

HAND BEARING COMPASS

FIGURE 11

43

for the compass, you have to add on the magnetic variation to your chart calculations.

CHART DATUM
The 'height' of the tide is the height that a high water reaches above a theoretical low water, known as 'chart datum'. Chart datum is the lowest predicted astronomical tide. On the chart, the depth of water (either in fathoms or feet, and more recently in metres) is always given as from chart datum. We'll come back to depth later.

COMPASSES
Marine compasses are not cheap, but they are a necessary investment. "Silva" have a very good range, at various prices.

When installing the compass in your boat you must bear two points in mind. Firstly it must be visible to the helm on any point of sailing, even when sitting out on a beat. Secondly, it must be installed where the deviation, that is, the attraction to the compass by metal objects in the boat, is minimised.

Dinghy sailors use *steering compasses* and *hand bearing compasses,* and both are useful. You can buy hand bearing compasses which can be fixed to a gimballed bracket for steering and unclipped and put into a handle socket when you need it to take a bearing on some landmark or buoy. Using a hand bearing compass in a dinghy is no easy task, for bearings must be taken quickly and you must avoid being too close to the attraction of wire shrouds. Fine accuracy is often not possible, or even necessary in a small boat, and a compass is only one (but a very important one) of the navigational aids you employ.

The easiest type of compass to steer by is the grid compass. As with everything else, one gets what one is prepared to pay for. A good one will be gimballed (i.e., it will stay horizontal and easily readable even when the dinghy heels). The grid is set on the desired course and the dinghy steered to keep the N.S. line on the card between the parallel wires of the T-shaped grid. Where to position this steering compass is an individual matter, different in each boat. Some have them sunk in the floorboards, others prefer them mounted on the centreboard casing, while others have them mounted flush in the side decks. Good visibility is of prime importance, so be sure you can see it.

TIDES AND CURRENTS

In a small sailing boat, working the tides is essential. It is useful to remember that tides run strongest in deep water, which is usually in the middle of the channel. Therefore, creep in shallow water along the edge of the estuary to cheat the tide a little if it is flowing against you.

FIGURE 12

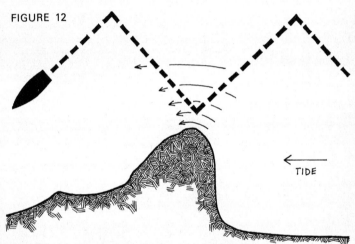

TIDE

TACK TO GAIN ADVANTAGE OF FAST CURRENT OFF HEADLAND

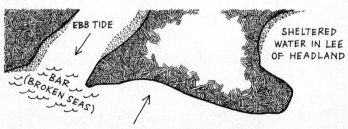

EBB TIDE

SHELTERED WATER IN LEE OF HEADLAND

BAR (BROKEN SEAS)

FRESH ONSHORE WIND

FIGURE 13

The outside bend of any channel will have the fastest flow of water, and often the inside bend will have a reverse eddy. Tides turn earliest around headlands and only later in the bays. For six hours or so, you may sail on flat water, with good stern winds but when the tides turn, the sea may get a lot rougher due to 'wind against tide' conditions. If this is realized you can plan to avoid it by consulting your tidal flow charts.

To travel long distances along the coast means using the tides to best advantage. Departing an hour before the tide turns in ones favour or even earlier than that, if the wind is fair, will give you a good start, because the '12ths rule' shows that even a foul tide against you is running much less strongly in the last two hours of its run. A favourable tide will turn first *inshore,* so you should hug the coast for the next six hours if possible, to avoid sitting out in a foul tide. Then the fair tide will help you longer if you then sail well out to sea, in the deep water, before it turns again inshore.

When the tide begins to turn, the surface shape of the waves begins to alter. 'Wind against tide' produces short, square, sloppy waves, and rough water may be expected over an uneven bottom or where two or more tides converge. Avoid plotting a course through such places if possible, and, if strong headwinds are encountered around headlands, then shelter may be found by hugging the shoreline, where smoother water and protection from the wind may be found. But remember that if the wind changes, you may be safer with some sea room between you and the headland. As you can see, there is a lot to consider.

When winds blow across oceans or large sea areas a 'big fetch' or swell can be set up. Arriving over sand banks the seas can be expected to be short, choppy and confused, but in a dinghy, you can creep behind sand banks into calm and sheltered waters at most states of the tide.

SPRINGS AND NEAPS

During 'springs' (at the new and full moon), tides are strongest, and you can expect faster ebbs, higher High-Water, and lower Low-Water. Neap tides (quarter and three-quarter moon phases) give a smaller range, less High-Water, and not so low Low-Water, and the tidal streams are less strong. Low atmospheric pressure, combined with a strong wind in the same direction as the main flood tide will result in a higher high-tide, standing later than predicted, and then a faster ebb-tide, so note that the weather affects the tides at all states.

TWELFTH'S RULE

As the tides flow and ebb the level of the water rises and falls. The strength of the tide depends on how near to High and Low water and how near to 'neaps' or 'springs' they are. By applying the 'Twelfth's Rule' the navigator can calculate the depth of water available for mooring and entering a river or estuary.

1st hour after H.W. or before L.W.—
difference = 1/12th of predicted tide
2nd hour after H.W. or before L.W.—
difference = 2/12ths of predicted tide
3rd hour after H.W. or before L.W.—
difference = 3/12ths of predicted tide
4th hour after H.W. or before L.W.—
difference = 3/12ths of predicted tide
5th hour after H.W. or before L.W.—
difference = 2/12ths of predicted tide
6th hour after H.W. or before L.W.—
difference = 1/12th of predicted tide

From this, it can be seen that the greatest rise or fall, and speed of tidal stream is in the middle two hours of the tide, and that the weakest strength and least movement is at the first and sixth hours of any tide. There are areas where the 12th's rule is less reliable, the double tide at Southampton being one example. So always check locally.

TIDE RIPS

If the cruise takes you around headlands where tide rips are marked, or over overfalls, it is important that these places should be passed at *slack water,* and never when the tide is turning against one. Some of the tide rips—for example around Portland Bill, can be quite violent for a small boat to travel through, even in good weather. Study the chart, for often an inshore passage is possible as well as an offshore one, and these inshore pasages are often the better way to go.

STEPS IN PLOTTING A COURSE

You will have no difficulty laying a course if you follow the following steps. You need a certain amount of information, either calculated or estimated, and apply it to your calculations.

The following steps will get you there.

1. Lay off the course with a pencil line on the chart, and find the true bearing by walking the rule over to the compass rose.

2. Consult tidal stream atlas and calculate effect of tidal stream on the course, as this may well affect the heading.

3. This will give you a true course, but to set this on the compass you need the magnetic bearing. To get this *add* the magnetic variation (obtained from the compass rose).

4. This will give you an effective magnetic course, but you then have to allow for leeway.

5. All sail powered craft make some leeway which is defined as the angle between the ship's fore and aft line and the wake. You can measure this with a hand bearing compass, or estimate it and allow for the magnetic course steered.

The diagram below (Fig. 14) may give you a calculation as follows:—

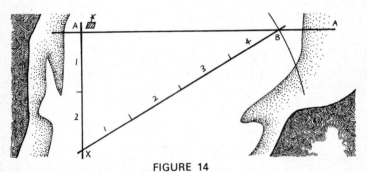

FIGURE 14

The direct course is 090° True. The magnetic variation is 7°. The tide is flowing 180°T at 2 Kts. The estimated leeway is 3°. The deviation on this heading is + 3°, and estimated speed 4 Kts.

1. Lay off a line for your true course A – A.

2. Using the latitude scale closest to your position, lay off 2 Kts. south of track (X).

3. Using the same scale from X measure off 4 Kts. along the track X to B.

4. Lay the parallel rules along XB, walk them over to the compass rose and you get a bearing 060°T.

Now you can do your sum:

True course to steer:	060°T
Plus magnetic variation 7°W	7°
	067°M
Plus deviation (or minus, depending on deviation on this heading)	+3
	070°M
Plus estimated leeway	3°
Steer compass course	073°M

Let me stress that this is just an example to show you the necessary steps, and not one taken from an actual cruise.

DEVIATION

Deviation is the local attraction to a compass needle by metal objects in the boat—like the mast, an engine or a can of beans, or outside—like a metal buoy. You must check the boat normally loaded, on all compass headings, to establish the compass deviation, plus or minus, on all points, and always beware of deviation and metal attraction.

LEEWAY

Leeway increases considerably when a yacht is close hauled, especially in short steep seas. It will vary according to the type of boat. A dinghy driven hard to windward with centreboard fully down will make little leeway. Reaching in a breaking sea, the crew may have to lift the centreboard to diminish the risk of the capsize, and the resultant leeway may be considerable. The amount of leeway and its direction will have to be estimated and allowed for in the calculation after setting off the effect of the tide. Leeway can be estimated by looking astern and estimating the angle of the wake in relation to the boat's heading, and applying this, expressed in degrees, to your calculations.

POSITION FINDING

Navigation at sea, in a small boat, is never easy. The basic work should be done long before one steps into the boat, because the violent motion of a boat in bad weather leads to situations where it is very easy to make mistakes.

FIXES

Every 'fix' depends upon an accurate position line, usually obtained by taking a bearing on some identifiable object on the shore, such as a church, water tower or lighthouse. After adding the magnetic variation and drawing this bearing on the chart, we know that our dinghy must be somewhere on that line. We then need to estimate our position along this line to obtain a position. Mark this on the chart with a cross, and put the time of the 'fix' beside it.

Sometimes, in poor visibility, one gets a glimpse of an object before the weather closes in, and this method therefore has its uses, but it isn't very accurate. A more accurate fix is obtained by taking a cross bearing on a second object, and where the second bearing crosses the first position line, this must be our position. (Try to take bearings on objects at approximately right angles to one another). The best method of all is to take bearings on three objects. (Try to get the fixes roughly at 60° angle to one another). Drawing these lines on to the chart you create a triangle, known as a 'cocked hat'. Putting a cross within the triangle, closest to any nearby hazard enables you to fix your position safely. Once again, the time should be noted and written on the chart beside the cross.

SPEED THROUGH THE WATER

Accurate estimates of your speed are essential. There are several methods of estimating speed. One way is to use a patent log, which consists of a rotator over the stern. This rotates a revolution counter on the stern. From the number of revolutions in a certain period, it is possible to work out the distance covered through the water. It can also be used to establish speed by noting the distance covered in a set period of time. Patent logs can be most useful, but they tend to under-read at slow speeds (i.e., less than 2 knots). They tend to over-register in strong headwinds. In shallow water they can collect weed which will again cause them to under-register.

Speed can be calculated by timing the passage of the dinghy past a floating object, (such as orange peel). There is also the "Dutchman's log". A member of the crew throws a floating object (not plastic please!) from the bows. The helmsman can see when it floats past the dinghy stern and its time noted. A calculation based on the time taken to pass the known length of the boat will give you a speed.

Another very good method for the dinghy cruiser is to watch any floating object go past his dinghy and then estimate the speed at

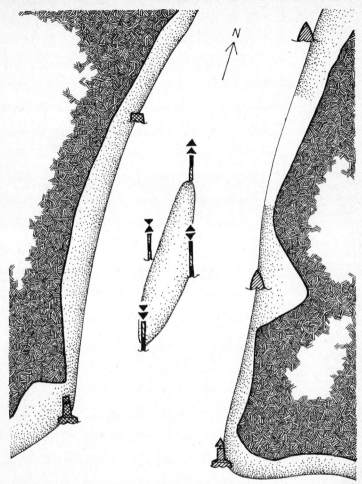

AN EXAMPLE OF I.A.L.A. SYSTEM A BUOYAGE.

FIGURE 15

 RED YELLOW GREEN

which he passes it, relative to his experience on land; i.e., a quick walk = about 4 knots; an afternoon stroll = about 2½ knots; a leisurely ramble = about 1½ knots. Providing the skipper knows his boat well, with experience, this method can be surprisingly accurate. However, it is unreliable at night, or in moonlight, or when tired or seasick.

DEPTH

In our *Wayfarer* we can get along in very shallow water with the centreboard up, but even in a dinghy, going aground on a falling tide can be a nuisance. Usually the centreboard coming up is the first sign that you are getting shallow. If you do go aground, get off quickly, putting the crew over to give you a push, or even give you a tow. Consult the charts and note the depths along your course. If it dries out you may have to plot another course to take you round the shallow area.

Navigation is fascinating, and great fun. If you use common-sense and approach the problems logically, it isn't even very difficult, so read it up, try out a few short trips first, plotting courses and bearings even when you know perfectly well where you are, until you build up experience and expertise, which brings me to the final rule of navigation. ALWAYS KNOW WHERE YOU ARE. There are all sorts of clues, and you must gather as many as you can. For example, you have (perhaps) the course you plotted, some recent fixes, a bearing you have just passed, another on the horizon, a ferry on a regular route, the wind on your cheek, the depth beneath the boat—all clues to finding your way about, and not only going somewhere, but—arriving!

Chapter 9

SEAMANSHIP

Dinghy cruising, in the normal course of events demands a high standard of seamanship and the regular use of skills which the racing helmsman has little need to employ. The dinghy cruising sailor is using his craft for its original purpose—going somewhere, and needs a range of techniques, some of which we have already discussed, if he is to get to his destination.

LAUNCHING, SAILING OFF

You must be very skilled in getting away from both lee and weather shores. With a laden boat, it is probably as well to row out, well offshore before hoisting sail, anchoring if necessary while doing so. Before leaving be sure you have left trolley and trailer somewhere secure, preferably padlocked. Have all gear checked on board and properly stowed, have a weather report, and, if appropriate, having informed the Coast Guard.

Starting a day cruise, it is a good idea to head upwind and uptide. Then, should things go wrong, you can easily get back to your car and trailer.

Think twice before going out in strong onshore winds, with a poor forecast, and avoid harbour bars unless you are *sure* they are safe, because once committed to crossing one, it is difficult to turn back. The cruising dinghy will usually find smoother water with offshore winds, even if they are strong.

LEE SHORES

Getting away from a lee shore means good team work. One can:—

1. Row out and anchor before putting up sails.
2. Insist that the crew stands offshore up to his waist in cold water while the main is hoisted, or better still,
3. Get the sails up, crew into the boat to attend to the centreboard while the helmsman gets in last, pushes off the shore and claws off using the main to edge into deep water before pulling in the jib sheets and sailing away.

Practise all these methods, never get wedded to one method, for no one way suits every situation.

TIME AND DISTANCE

The scope for dinghy cruising is vast, but before setting out you must:—

1. Know where you are going.
2. Know how far it is.
3. Have calculated the time necessary to get there.
4. Have an alternative destination in mind, if things don't work out as planned.

The dinghy sailor must use the tides. Careful study of tide tables can make or mar your trip.

Even with the best-found craft, experienced crew and well-formed plans, things go wrong, so let's just look at a few possibilities.

JURY RIG

On some calm day it tests the initiative of the boat owner to consider how he could improvise in a real emergency. If the mast broke, an oar could be lashed in its place. If the rudder snapped off, another oar could be lashed to the transom to make a steering device. If the centreboard broke, perhaps a floorboard could be substituted, or even lashed over the side to form an elementary leeboard. A broken boom is no tragedy, as a loose footed main is reasonably efficient. If a bottlescrew or shackle fails or the shrouds part the boat should be put on the other tack while a repair is effected. You must speculate on these problems and solutions. It helps to have some idea of what to do.

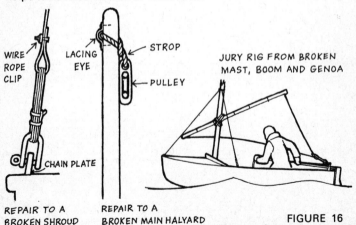

WIRE ROPE CLIP

LACING EYE

STROP

PULLEY

JURY RIG FROM BROKEN MAST, BOOM AND GENOA

CHAIN PLATE

REPAIR TO A BROKEN SHROUD

REPAIR TO A BROKEN MAIN HALYARD

FIGURE 16

TOWING

A tow is something everybody is glad of at some time. The towing warp should be wrapped around the mast, samson post or thwart, and secured with a slip knot. The warp should then be led through the fairlead and the weight (the crew) in the boat kept towards the stern. For a long tow, the sails should be taken down, the centreboard should be nearly completely up. An ideal speed for towing is 3 knots. It gets unpleasant and uncomfortable over 8 knots. Be sure whoever offers the tow is aware of these limitations. In a choppy sea the tow line can be weighted to act as a shock absorber. It is very important to be sure that the tow rope does not jump out of the fairlead. You may even have to lash it in, but just be sure it stays there.

MAN OVERBOARD

This always happens when least expected, often in the calmest conditions. Even in two-foot waves, a head is invisible to the helmsman, and so the place where the accident happened must be kept in sight. Gybing round may result in two people being in the water instead of one, and so, even although gybing effects a quicker turn, the safer method is to sail off on a broad reach, under main only, with jib flying, and 'going about' to approach the area on a reciprocal reach. Pick them up on the windward side of the boat, making certain that the boat carries 'no way' when the helm leaves the tiller to help his mate aboard at the shrouds. By hooking a foot and an elbow over the gunwhales the "overboard" can roll in as the boat is heeled back again. An alternative plan is to let him climb over the transom with a foot in a loop of the mainsheet. If the person in the water is unconscious you can only tie him beneath the armpits and hope to haul him aboard by main force. He may be shocked and cold and not able to help, and so, as a last resort, all you can do is to tie him, face uppermost, to the boat and sail him ashore.

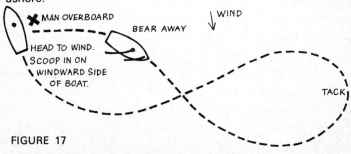

FIGURE 17

ANCHORING TIPS

When coming ashore, aim to land at high water, as this avoids humping gear over soft mud. If you have a tender, you can anchor in deep water and leave the dinghy afloat out there if it is *certain* that she will not dry out, on a rocky bottom, a few hours later. If sleeping on board, anchor on the inside bend of the river, with sufficient scope between shore and channel to ensure that the late evening is not spent in the deep channel or at an alarming angle up the river bank. In restricted channels one should moor fore and aft to avoid swinging. Never anchor in deep water channels where there is a lot of shipping, and a riding light, such as a lantern, must be hung in the shrouds if there are other boats about. Picking up a mooring saves tending anchor lines when the tides turn, but before using it, check with the harbour-master that it can be used, and that it is secure. Picking up either a mooring buoy or anchoring takes practice, and the dinghy sailor is never wasting a nice afternoon if he uses it to practise this manoeuvre. You need to consider whether the tide and wind are together or against one another, and at what strength both are running. Study your charts for good anchorages and also spoiled ground. In uncertain or on foul ground it is safer to buoy the anchor, and always, in unfamiliar harbours, put a tripping line on it, so that should the bottom be foul, you have a better chance of freeing it in the morning.

You may want to anchor the dinghy offshore, while sleeping ashore. There are two ways of doing this, while still being able to recover the boat without swimming out to it—provided you have two warps, or a good length of line.

1. Lay the anchor, on the foredeck, with the warp coiled and belayed. Tie your line to the crown of the anchor with a fisherman's bend, and shove the boat out into deep water, paying out line as it goes. At the appropriate spot jerk the anchor off the foredeck. Remember that you must belay the anchor warp on board allowing sufficient line, but only sufficient line for anchoring at that spot. You don't want the boat drifting ashore as all the warp runs out. Tie your line to some secure point and in the morning you can drag anchor and boat inshore.

2. Untie the warp from the anchor, and shackle a spare block in its place. Lead the warp through the block on the anchor, then drop the anchor over. Now row ashore, easing out the warp. When you have unloaded, you haul the boat out to her anchor, and belay the warp ashore. Ease the line in the morning, and the boat should drift ashore.

CAPSIZE

If reefing was done in good time, many a capsize could be averted, but when it does happen, especially in and around U.K. waters, exposure must be considered because in sea temperatures below 40°F survival time is frighteningly short. A person keeping still in the water will not cool down as quickly as one swimming or flapping around, but it is still better to right the boat as speedily as possible. If the boat—a loaded dinghy, remember—will not come up on the first go, lower the sails and try again. Finally, failing to do this, fully inflate the life jacket, tie yourself to the boat, keep as still as possible in the water and await help. If no help is available, keep trying. Learn and practise capsize drills regularly.

CAPSIZE DRILL

To right the dinghy, the helmsman, holding on to the mainsheet, should swim round to the centreboard and climb on to it, keeping his weight close to the hull of the boat. The crew, to help him, throws a jib sheet over the hull to him, as with it the helmsman can use extra leverage to climb up the outside of the boat. The crew can talk to one another through the centreboard. As the boat comes upright—hopefully aided by the tide if the dinghy is lying down tide—the crew, positioning himself along the shrouds should be scooped up inside the boat. From there, he can help his skipper in with him, and start bailing. If the boat is in danger of turning turtle, everybody should let go of it. Once inverted, the seal with the water has then to be broken, before you can right it. A good preventive measure is to attach a hollow fender to the mast tip.

A capsize while cruising is to be dreaded. There may be no one to help, and it is far, far, better to have a stable boat, have it correctly loaded and rigged and reef very early. Always beware of a capsize when cruising. Righting a boat inshore is a different kettle of fish from doing it on the open sea.

HEAVING TO [Fig. 18]

This is a means of slowing down the dinghy to allow the fleet to catch up, let everyone have a rest, or do repairs or have a meal. For short stops, the dinghy can be brought on to a broad reach and the sails then allowed to 'let fly'. For longer stops, the boat should be luffed into the wind and stopped. A transit with two objects on shore will tell you when this has happened. The balance of the sails holding the dinghy head to wind, with the jib cleated tight aback, and the main loosened off, with the tiller hard down, and the centreboard half up, should result in the dinghy lying quietly,

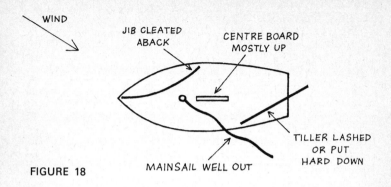

WIND

JIB CLEATED ABACK

CENTRE BOARD MOSTLY UP

TILLER LASHED OR PUT HARD DOWN

MAINSAIL WELL OUT

FIGURE 18

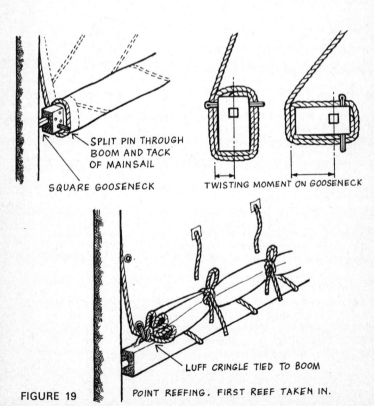

SPLIT PIN THROUGH BOOM AND TACK OF MAINSAIL

SQUARE GOOSENECK

TWISTING MOMENT ON GOOSENECK

LUFF CRINGLE TIED TO BOOM

FIGURE 19

POINT REEFING. FIRST REEF TAKEN IN.

merely drifting on the tide, at about one knot. Until one is experienced, reefing afloat is best done in a 'hove to' position.

REEFING

This can be done progressively by substituting a smaller set of sails, for example, by lowering the genoa and reefing the main, and, finally, sailing under reefed main only. Roller reefing, using reefing ties or the jiffy reefing system, are all methods of achieving the same purpose—which is to reduce the sail area and prevent your craft being overpowered in strong winds. To achieve a good shape when rolling in a reef, the lower batten should be removed from the pocket in the main sail. When reefing the crew should always be to windward, and the boat hove to.

COMING ASHORE

Leeshores: Approaching windward shores presents few problems, but a change to an onshore wind can make landing a dangerous time. Heaving to, at least 50 yards offshore, upwind of the selected landing place, to size up the situation is a sensible thing to do. (The same applies when approaching a bar.) The main can be lowered, you can sail closer to the shore under jib, and, finally, pull up the centreboard and run in to shore under jib alone at a slow speed. Alternatively both sails can be lowered, and you can row in. If conditions look really bad, the dinghy can be anchored over the bow and backed in, rudder removed, using the oars for control. Another method is to use a bucket towed over the stern to slow one down and hold the boat as you row ashore. Practise these methods on good days, so that you and your crew establish a routine. Don't wait for a bad day.

Windward Shores: The rule of stopping for a look holds good in this situation as well. Unless you know the area well, you don't want to storm in close hauled, or on a fast reach, although to get inshore at all you may have to. You can drop the sails and row in, and for a rocky anchorage this is advisable. Study the chart for depth, and obstructions, and if you go in with the sails up, have the crew ready to back the jib and go over with the painter to hold you on while you drop the main. Don't send him over clutching the anchor, into 20 feet of water! Wait till the boat is definitely in shallow water, then luff up and let the sheets fly. Here again, this is a situation you can practise any afternoon, and it does take practise and co-ordination between the crew.

TIPS ON ROUGH WEATHER HELMSMANSHIP

Skill in rough weather helming will be needed at some point. When beating into bad seas, you must be prepared to *luff* into the breaking wave, but *pay off* directly afterwards to avoid losing speed and control. Look out for squalls, luffing into them, and let the main well out if the gust looks like being a prolonged one. Over-reefing can mean that in the deep troughs between the seas, you lose the wind, and therefore the speed necessary for control.

Beating in rough water, wait for a calm patch before going about and always get the boat sailing fast before doing so. With the mainsheet hauled in hard, when the dinghy is spun broadside on to a sea, and with little way on her, she may not go about. All you can do then is to sit out hard and release the pressure on the main. If the centreboard is right down she may trip over it, so it is important to slide it up a little. When reaching, putting the centreboard down will reduce weather helm, especially if the crew shifts his weight aft.

Running before a big sea can be a frightening experience. When the dinghy wants to run off the wind and lie over in the trough, broaching can be guarded against, by reducing sail and keeping the transom of the dinghy at *exactly right angles* to each sea. This calls for careful steering. Accidental gybes in big running seas must not occur, and in these conditions, to run with twin jibs set instead of a main can mean a much steadier sail. If planing downwind gets a bit too exciting, tack on a broad reach, going about at each corner instead of gybing.

Clearly, if you are going to cruise in a dinghy, you must anticipate being caught out sometime. Take every precaution you can, but should you get caught, then keep calm and concentrate. The boat will look after you if you give it a chance.

SEA ANCHOR

If the seas get really bad, you may have to take in all sail, and even take the mast down as well, to reduce windage, and lie to a sea-anchor.

A sea-anchor resembles a windsock, and is, basically, a drogue. It should be made of terylene, and each seam, mouth and base, should be reinforced with terylene rope. Stream this anchor over the bow, putting out a length of warp at least five times longer than the boat, and lie to it until the weather moderates.

RUNNING AGROUND

Centreboard boats suffer little if they run aground on a soft bottom. You can always get out and push off, and usually the centreboard touches first and gives you good warning. It would not be a good idea to run aground hard, all standing, the strain on the standing rigging might be too much. If the wind is off the shore just back the jib, bring the weight aft and let the wind push you off.

Don't be afraid to get out and tow the boat into deeper water, or to get the oars out and row—an act that usually calls up the wind like magic.

Guard against beating into shallow waters with the centreboard right down as to touch bottom may cause a capsize.

NIGHT PASSAGES

Sometimes night passages are easier than day trips, because offshore breezes may be steadier, and problem headwinds often die away at dusk. It is often necessary to sail before dawn, in order to catch a tide, or reach one's destination in daylight.

Start learning about night sailing by some evening cruises, aiming to come in before it gets really dark. You will need to study lights, on buoys and passing ships, and learn some quite new techniques for coastal navigation. Remember that your boat must carry lights.

Those who start night sailing seem to enjoy it, and I would urge you not to reject it out of hand, or to begin it without adequate preparation.

SHIPPING LANES

Stay out of shipping lanes. Your shallow draft enables you to keep in shoal water, out of the main channels, so do so. If you have to cross a shipping lane do so at right angles, and hold a steady course, without flapping around, confusing the helmsman of some oncoming ship.

GENERALLY IN CRUISING KEEP AWAY FROM THE SHORE EXCEPT:

SMALL DINGHYS STAY INSHORE —
1. IN FOG.
2. HEAVY RAIN SQUALLS AND POOR VISIBILITY.
3. IN LIGHT WINDS WHEN MANŒUVREBILITY
   IS LIMITED

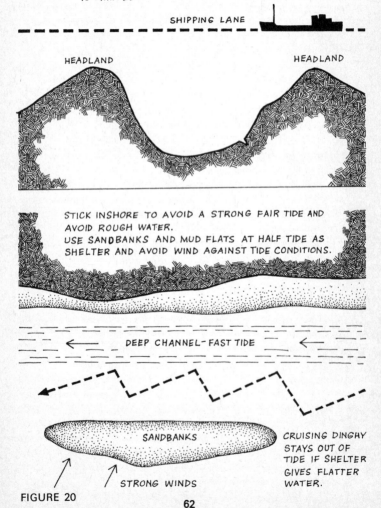

SHIPPING LANE

HEADLAND   HEADLAND

STICK INSHORE TO AVOID A STRONG FAIR TIDE AND
AVOID ROUGH WATER.
USE SANDBANKS AND MUD FLATS AT HALF TIDE AS
SHELTER AND AVOID WIND AGAINST TIDE CONDITIONS.

DEEP CHANNEL–FAST TIDE

SANDBANKS

STRONG WINDS

CRUISING DINGHY
STAYS OUT OF
TIDE IF SHELTER
GIVES FLATTER
WATER.

FIGURE 20

Chapter 10

PLANNING A CRUISE

By now, you may feel that dinghy cruising is a lot of work and that you need a whole new range of skills and equipment to even start. Well, everyone has to start somewhere, so let's end this book by organising your first cruise.

To begin with I recommend that you cruise in company with either the cruising section of your own Class Association, or on cruises organized by the Dinghy Cruising Association. You join, announce the wish to go on a particular cruise that attracts you, and you will receive a full range of information on kit and experience required, meeting places and times of launch. Going on a few of these trips will teach you a lot, introduce you to many new friends and resolve a lot of problems.

When eventually it comes to planning your own cruise, may I suggest this list as a step-by-step routine, for you to follow:

1. Obtain charts of and maps to the chosen area. Read and study any available information, in cruising guides or yachting books. Study tide tables and tidal flow charts. Is it a suitable place for that weekend?

2. Consult handbooks for launching site information (Getting Afloat).

3. If applicable book a camp site (2 weeks before at least) longer in summer. Study tide tables (Reeds Almanac).

4. Prepare complete list of stores, and have the crew check it.

5. Arrange car parking place and secure storage for trolley and trailer.

6. Work out the courses for each leg of your cruise, using all available information. Have the crew check you calculations and then write them down clearly—with timings (one week before).

7. Three days before start, assemble weather information and prepare forecasts. Check trailer and trolley, lights and tyres.

8. The day before (a) check boat, hull and rigging, (b) have all stores ready to pack, (c) ring weather centre for local forecast, (d) prepare form for Coast Guard.

9. Before departure: Load stores, checking as you do so. Strap down boat on trailer. Obtain weather forecast. Check trailer lights. Depart.

10. On journey: After 10 miles stop and check load and lashings.

11. On arrival: A. Reach launch site, talk to locals for any advice on your intended cruise. B. Load and rig boat, advise Coast Guard. Obtain latest forecast. C. Launch. Wash off the trolley wheels in fresh water.

12. Park car and trolley with trailer, somewhere secure, and off you go!

On return, apart from advising the Coast Guard of your safe return, and thanking any club for their facilities, the important thing is to recover the boat carefully on to the trolley, and note any repairs to hull or rigging necessary before your next trip.

Wash down the boat and muddy gear with fresh water before heading home. The trip will dry it nicely. Carry out all your routine checks, as listed above, on the trolley, trailer and lashings. Don't let tiredness and the hurry to get home make you careless.

All this is, believe me, part of the fun. You're going on a VOYAGE! and the preparation is part of the thrill.

STOP OR GO

When you get to your launch site, you may have to make the decision, in the face of weather conditions, on whether to go or not.

If in doubt, launch and go out and have a look. Often it doesn't seem half as bad out there as it looks from the shore. This is especially so if the forecast says the weather is moderating. However if the forecast offers only more of the same, or worsening weather then pocket your pride and come in again. You can probably do some day sailing, or practise some manoeuvres, so the trip need not be wasted.

CONCLUSION

This has been a practical book, and I have tried to include, or refer you to all the points I think you should know before you go cruising in a small boat. Space has not permitted me to cover the excitement, or fun, or sense of adventure, but they are an integral part of dinghy cruising. But then, I'm sure you would prefer to find that out for yourself!